LEOPARD TORTOISE GUIDE

The Complete Beginners Guide On How to Take Care of Leopard Tortoise as Pet. (Leopard Tortoise Care, Housing, Handling, Behavior Feeding and Health Care)

Jack Miller

TABLE OF CONTENT

Chapter one: Leopard Tortoise Description and behavioral aspect

There are two diagnosed leopard tortoise subspecies: the southern (S. p. pardalis) and the northern (S. p. babcocki). The variety of the latter inside Africa is Sudan, east to Ethiopia and Somalia, down the jap aspect of Africa to the Southern Cape and back up the western aspect to Angola. Stigmochelys p. paralysis is confined to the southern part of South Africa and Namibia. The two subspecies will readily interbreed if housed collectively, generating feasible offspring.

Leopard tortoises typically inhabit dry grassland areas and are regarded to arise in low densities for the duration of their large variety. They've considered meals object with the aid of many indigenous African human beings and some populations are prone. Despite the fact that the best two subspecies are identified, there is a tremendous deal of variability in length, pattern, and even form within localized populations, with possible undescribed subspecies present.

Adult leopards are high-domed tortoises that variety in duration from 10 to 21 inches, and that can weigh as much as 45 kilos. Stigmochelys p. babcocki is the most readily available leopard tortoise within the puppy exchange, with men averaging 10 inches and women 12 to sixteen inches. There are reviews of notably big specimens from South Africa and Ethiopia that weigh nicely over 70 kilos.

There is lots of colour variation in leopard tortoises. They generally have a golden carapace covered with black flecking or spots. Every sample is like a fingerprint and unique to that tortoise. The pardalis subspecies is thought to be a darker form, less domed, and grows to a larger size. Hatchlings may be distinguishable from babcocki hatchlings because they generally (now not always, but) have spots in line with scute, and babcocki hatchlings have one or none.

The leopard tortoise is found inside the savannas of Jap and Southern Africa, from Sudan to the southern

Cape of the continent and is the most broadly disbursed tortoise in Southern Africa. They are a grazing species of tortoise that favors semi-arid, thorny to grassland habitats, despite the fact that a few leopard tortoises have been found in rainier areas.

A completely lengthy-lived animal, the leopard tortoise reaches sexual adulthood between the whole of 12 and 15 years. Captive leopard tortoises, but, grow faster and can mature as younger as 6 years of age. Leopard tortoises the "courtroom" by using the male ramming the lady while mating, the male makes grunting vocalizations. After mating, the woman lays and seize inclusive of five to 18 eggs.

Leopard tortoises are extra protective than offensive, retracting feet and head into their shell for protection.

This frequently consequences in a hissing sound, likely because of the squeezing of air from the lungs as the limbs and head are retracted.

Chapter two: Classification and Toxonomy of Leopard Lizard

"How I stay there"

Leopard tortoises are nicely tailored to the semi-arid situations of the savannah and do not tolerate damp or bloodless nicely. Their days are geared to the fluctuating temperatures in their arid surroundings. As with every arid area, the African savannah stories hot temperature fluctuations over a 24-hour length. It gets particularly warm in the course of the day when the solar is burning brightest but cools off significantly when the sun is going down. Leopard tortoises are most energetic early within the morning and simply before the solar is going down, whilst the temperature is maximum mild. They are seeking refuge at some point in the most up to date part of the day and fall asleep early to avoid the cold.

While awake, leopard tortoises spend maximum in their time grazing on combined grasses. Like other turtles and tortoises, they haven't any ears but can sense vibrations that assist them to navigate their surroundings. They have an eager feel of odor that possibly facilitates them to discover meals. They haven't any teeth (no turtle or tortoise does); however, they chunk and rip at meals with their difficult, sharp, beak-like mouths. Leopard tortoises also consume the fruit and pads of prickly pear cactus and other succulents that provide them with water. They keep water in big anal sacs that take up most of the distance of their abdominal cavities. This is an essential physical adaptation to their arid environment.

"Making my mark"

Leopard tortoises are a signature animal of the African savannah and are one of the maximum hit species in this habitat. They're stunning tortoises without difficulty identified by means of their domed carapaces with contrasting black and yellow patterns. (The shell's pinnacle is the carapace. The shell's bottom is the plastron.)

Distinguishing a male leopard tortoise from a girl can be difficult on sight, even though adult males normally develop larger than women. The most important leopard tortoises on file have measured over two toes long and weigh about 80 pounds, but those are uncommon giants of the species.

Elevating young

Turtles and tortoises don't exactly "enhance young." They aren't huge on parental involvement. Adult males exit the scene after mating. Females excavate nests, lay their eggs, cowl them up, and leave. Mating season itself is an energetic time, though, with male and girl leopard tortoises becoming alternatively competitive. Women and men will butt and ram different tortoises with which they're competing for pals.

Leopard tortoises nest among May additionally and October. Ladies dig a nest approximately 10-30 cm deep and lay from 5-30 eggs at a time. Leopard tortoise eggs incubate for a prolonged but variable period, ranging from approximately five months to over a year. While equipped to hatch, each hatchling has a small egg tooth that it makes use of to break out of its shell. Leopard tortoise hatchlings are brightly patterned at birth, and entirely on their personal. They straight away start to feed on a spread of plant life, but seem to decide upon succulents, possibly due to the better water content.

Chapter three: To make a Leopard Tortoise as pet

Choosing an awesome Leopard Tortoise

Leopard tortoises can be purchased from a puppy store, reptile display, or maybe on the net, however, I advise selecting a tortoise in-person to keep away from problems. Whilst selecting a leopard tortoise, select one with excellent strong weight and a tough, firm shell, and one that appears sturdy and alert. You need a tortoise with clean eyes; clear, easy nostrils, and a smooth vent. Tortoises which can be light in weight or with partially closed or puffy eyes, a skinny or broken shell, nasal discharge, or runny stools must be averted.

Leopard Tortoise Breeding

Leopard tortoises are typically bred in captivity. Men can be prominent from females through their longer, thicker tails. Men additionally broaden a concavity to their plastrons, which aids them whilst mounting a lady. Girls have shorter tails and do no longer expand the concave plastrons visible in adult males. Well-fed men, raised on a wholesome diet, mature at around five years of age and girls at 7 years.

Leopard tortoise girls can lay eggs year-round. My leopards start breeding right here in Arizona in April or May additionally and could breed all through the year. Women will start laying in August or September and keep till February.

Women usually turn out to be stressed inside the days before they deposit their eggs, and they will tempo the enclosure and even dig a few take a look at holes within the days before they certainly nest. They will then lay 3 to 5 clutches a season, with a grasp laid every four to 6 weeks. The average grasps size degrees from 12 to 20 eggs. Leopard tortoise eggs left inside the floor in Phoenix, Ariz., will hatch out of the ground in August of the following year, generally after a rain. But, to defend the eggs from predators and excessive temperatures, I pull them from the nests and incubate them interiorly.

Clutches pulled for incubation require diapauses (a cooling duration) before incubation. To offer this, I hold the eggs in a 65-degree wine cooler for one month. They're then eliminated from the cooler and positioned in an incubator at the stop of the cooling month, wherein they normally incubate for 4 months at 84 to 86 stages Fahrenheit with a humidity degree of 60 percent. Eggs incubated at cooler temperatures will nevertheless hatch, however it takes longer.

Incubation takes six to 10 months; with eggs from the identical seize hatching at varying durations, even months aside. A hatchling pips the eggshell with a caruncle, or egg enamel, at the tip of its nostril. Once the egg is piped, the hatchling will often rest internal for some hours, to as lots as a day, earlier than it pushes its manner out of the egg. As soon as out, it'll feed on yolk final in its machine for multiple days

Then it will feed on finely shredded veggies.

Preserving Hatchling Leopard Tortoises indoors

Hatchlings may be housed in a 20-gallon "long" terrarium measuring 12 through 12 via 24 inches lengthy. I can preserve six clean hatchlings in a 20 long until they're 2 inches in duration, at which point I decrease the wide variety to 4 according to enclosure until they measure four inches. At 4 inches I both pass them to a tub (including a Water land tub) or a blanketed outside pen of similar dimensions. Create a hotspot within the indoor hatchling enclosure, in addition to a temperature gradient, by positioning an underneath-tank heater (available in shops that promote puppy reptile components) and/or a highlight at one end of the enclosure.

At some point in the day, the hotter quit has to reach 90 ranges Fahrenheit, even as the alternative, cooler stop ought to be maintained in the mid-80s. Middle of the night temperatures can drop to the mid-70s during the enclosure.

Leopard tortoises require vitamin D3 to a method and soak up calcium, and that is commonly furnished through direct exposure to natural daylight, UVB mild, and/or nutritional supplementation. Hatchlings housed interior will require a terrific, complete-spectrum UVB mild over the enclosure, and it needs to continue to be illuminated for 12 to fourteen hours an afternoon.

There are numerous options for substrates for younger tortoises saved indoors. Newspaper, Bermuda grass, rabbit pellets, and cypress mulch have all been used efficaciously, but I like peat moss mixed with sand at a 60/forty ratio. Cedar mulches or sand by means of itself have to be prevented.

A loss of humidity may be a contributing cause of pyramiding, a shell deformity that occurs whilst a tortoise is saved too dry and/or offered a flawed weight-reduction plan. I lessen the threat of this disfiguring increase by means of maintaining the peat and sand substrate moistened (now not wet) on the hotter end of the enclosure, with a cover located over the west region. This provides extra humidity in dry weather.

A shallow water dish that allows tortoises to effortlessly climb inside and outside must be supplied. A plastic plant saucer driven down into the substrate works properly

Small Petri dishes and different flat saucers can be used, too. I also automatically soak my tortoise hatchlings in a shallow dish of lukewarm water for 20 minutes each couple of days.

It's critical to keep away from a steady hot temperature with dry situations during the entire enclosure, as doing so will purpose a negative environment for elevating hatchlings. Offer a gradient and humidity. Hatchlings will develop on common 2 to 4 inches a yr. As noted, when mine attains 4 inches they'll be moved to a protected outside the enclosure. The pen should be protected with screening or different strategies, due to the fact smaller tortoises are clean objectives for dogs, cats, raccoons, opossums, foxes, fire ants, and even massive birds.

Out- doors Pens for Adults

Leopard tortoises do not dig burrows and alternatively are looking for a safe haven in bushes or low brush. Therefore, they are now not as damaging as a number of the other larger species of tortoises, making them desirable for landscaped again yards. Due to the fact they do no longer hibernate, however, leopard tortoises do require supplemental heat inside the winter while night temperatures drop beneath 60 levels Fahrenheit. a cold environment, and particularly one that is bloodless and damp, can be deadly to puppy leopard tortoises.

Adults can be housed out of doors in warmer, drier climates in pens crafted from concrete blocks, fence panels, or staked 14- to 16-inch wood rails. Those substances offer a visual barrier and are higher acceptable to a tortoise enclosure than mesh or chain-hyperlink fencing, which they'll try to push through. Avoid which include any sandy or rocky regions within the pen, as leopard tortoises may also ingest such substrate even as consuming, causing impaction. Maximum keepers of massive tortoises feed their tortoises on grassy regions, or they vicinity the meals (a various salad of chopped vegetables and greens) on large plastic trays.

Leopard tortoises like to wander, so they should be saved in out of doors pens which might be as big as viable, with 12 feet with the aid of 12 toes the minimal length for an unmarried grownup. A 16- by the 20-foot pen can house a trio or 4 adults. I have saved multi-male and woman groups of two men and 6 women without a male preventing problems, but this turned into a pen measuring forty by using forty toes. Nevertheless, I have no longer located male leopards to be large opponents. In fact, I currently house an opposite trio of pardalis adult males and one girl together without problems.

Shade timber or bushes can be planted in the pen to provide cowl. Grass must be planted to offer natural browse for the tortoises to devour. the maximum will drink standing water from a shallow dish or plant saucer. A cover box or shelter can be offered in addition to the shrubbery of their enclosure, and this conceals field can be heated with a ceramic or infrared warm bulb or pig blanket whilst temperatures drop beneath 60 tiers at night, as well as when daylight temperatures drop beneath 70 ranges.

The correct foods

I feed our leopard tortoises a high-fiber food regimen each day. Adult tortoises are allowed to graze on a greater natural weight loss program of Bermuda grass and will want much less supplemental foods. I offer dried grasses together with timothy hay or a Bermuda grass blend with a few alfalfas to both indoor and outside tortoises. I feed an expansion of supplemental foods inclusive of vegetables together with romaine, dandelions, or an extraordinary spring blend without spinach. I keep away from ingredients that are high in oxalic acids, including chard, spinach, and rhubarb. Oxalic acids bind with calcium, which prevents the tortoise from soaking up the calcium. I do upload vegetables together with zucchini, carrots, bell peppers, and squashes. Leopard tortoises additionally like grape and mulberry tree leaves, in addition to Opuntia cactus pads and succulents. I avoid any fruits, citrus or acidic veggies which include tomatoes. I also do no longer feed my tortoise's canned dog or cat ingredients and meat.

Vegetables must be dusted with a super nutrition powder and calcium powder once a week. For hatchlings kept interior, a calcium powder with D3 needs to be used. Many tortoise keepers additionally add cuttlebone to their tortoise enclosures, which the tortoises will chew on, receiving extra calcium within the manner. A business herbivore tortoise weight loss plan also can be presented to complement your tortoise's primary weight loss plan of grasses.

Viable fitness problems

Properly husbandry practices together with those described in this article will assist keep away from or prevent health issues. In any other case, a number of the following situations may be skilled.

Leopard tortoises kept in cool, moist climates may suffer from top respiratory infections. Parasites, including worms and flagellates, can also present fitness troubles for leopard tortoises. If swollen eyes, a runny nostril, runny stool, or lack of urge for food occurs, a session with a terrific reptile veterinarian is recommended.

Tortoises can also become infected by viruses and bacterial infections. Many can be providers of viruses lengthy before they showcase any signs. New tortoises must consequently be quarantined away from current animals for at least 30 to 90 days to save you exposing them to new viruses.

I advocate no longer blending species inside a tortoise series, and having new additions checked by way of a qualified reptile veterinarian for the duration of their quarantine duration.

Leopard tortoises are one of the maximum attractive and appealing tortoises inside the reptile-maintaining interest. They have a great temperament and are long-lived, and they may be a less detrimental species that remains a manageable size for most tortoise keepers. If you want tortoises, you'll love having a leopard tortoise.

Chapter four: How to maintain the captive habitat

If you live in a cold climate, you can want to rethink owning a leopard tortoise. These animals need hot temperatures 12 months-spherical and have no tolerance for the cold. Because of its size and need for daylight, leopard tortoises have to be stored in a safe, outdoor enclosure as tons as possible.

In case you plan to have a leopard tortoise on your yard, its enclosure ought to have an area where it is able to hide. It wishes to be fenced-in to help the tortoise experience comfortable and to protect it from predators. Do no longer residence a leopard tortoise wherein even a well-which means dog, may encounter it; the state of affairs won't give up well for the tortoise. Tortoise hatchlings, for his or her first months of life, have to remain housed interior away from predators.

Make its enclosure like its natural habitat. Provide alfalfa and other grasses for it to graze on. Maintain a shallow pan of water available for drinking, but make certain the tortoise does not get caught in it.

Within the wild, tortoises dig within the dirt to put eggs, so offer the naked floor for digging in its pen. Solar exposure is important for leopard tortoises and therefore needs a basking area where they could soak up vitamin D, which is critical for the right fitness.

If you can't hold your tortoise outdoors 12 months-rounds, be organized to build a substantial indoor pen: an enclosure this is as a minimum 10 feet by using 10 ft with walls at the least 2 ft excessive. When you have a small spare room in a warm vicinity of your own home, bear in mind changing it into a tortoise haven.

Spot smooth the tortoise's indoor or outdoor enclosure with the aid of getting rid of visible puppy wastes and clean out its water dish day by day.

Warmness

As cold-blooded creatures, all reptiles need to alter their frame temperature. Ideally, daylight temperatures must be between 80 F and ninety F, and midnight temperatures must not pass beneath sixty-five F. Leopard tortoises can't tolerate cooler or damp situations. offer a basking location that reaches 95 F. if you're housing the animal indoors, use reptile heat bulbs or ceramic heater emitters to mimic these temperatures and encompass a temperature gradient.

Light

Leopard tortoises thrive in direct sunlight. Seeing that a leopard tortoise housed indoors does now not get direct daylight, a full-spectrum ultraviolet mild is important. This specialized, UVB light needs to shine immediately at the tortoise (no longer filtered through glass or plastic) 10 to 12 hours a day

If indoors, also offer a basking light that shines down on a basking spot, together with flat rocks that hold warmth.

Humidity

Relative humidity of forty percent to 60 percent is right for leopard tortoises at some point of the day. These tortoises opt for 70 percent to 80 percent relative humidity at night time, which may be completed by way of misting the substrate at night time. Take a look at moisture tiers with a hygrometer or humidity gauge placed within the cage.

Substrate

Most pet owners use a substrate or bedding to line the bottom of an enclosure. In case your leopard tortoise lives in most cases outside, where it can dig inside the dust and forage at the grass, a secondary indoor enclosure can use newspapers for the substrate. Trade the newspaper liner often.

If your leopard tortoise's enclosure is often interior, provide a grass or hay substrate or an organic soil-sand mixture to offer the texture of its natural habitat.

Food and Water

The Leopard tortoises are known to be herbivorous grazers, they feed majorly throughout the day. About 50 to 80 percent of their diet must be comprised of excessive-fiber grasses and veggies. Outdoor pesticide-unfastened grass is appropriate for grazing in the course of warm climate. Their day by day weight loss plan needs to consist ordinarily of timothy grass or hay. Each day, at the equal time every day, you may feed small amounts of other veggies (dandelion vegetables, collard veggies, watercress, carrots) on a bed of timothy hay.

Feed the number of meals they may eat within 15 to 30 minutes. The rule of thumb is to offer a quantity of approximately the size of the tortoise's shell.

Keep away from feeding leopard tortoise leafy veggies that are excessive in oxalates, consisting of beet veggies, Swiss chard, and spinach.

These veggies and fruits can cause digestive issues and diarrhea, which could result in dehydration. By no means feed canine meals, cat food, or some other animal protein in your leopard tortoise. These foods can harm a tortoise's kidneys.

An indoor tortoise requires extra vitamins to make up for its lack of direct sunlight. Supply your pet a brilliant tortoise food that includes calcium and nutrition D3 dietary supplements. Tortoises can gnaw on pieces of cuttlebone, which can be discovered inside the hen segment of maximum pet shops, to sell beak health and offer greater calcium.

Chapter five: Some common health issues of Leopard Tortoise

Captive leopard tortoises are noticeably at risk of breathing infections. Those normally arise while the animal's enclosure is too humid. Every other common and painful situation amongst tortoises is shell rot, which is due to fungal contamination. Symptoms of shell rot encompass a dry, flaky shell that can have a foul smell.

Possibly the maximum extreme disorder that afflicts captive leopard tortoises is a metabolic bone ailment. This probably deadly situation effects from an imbalance in the tortoise's phosphorous-to-calcium ratio. The metabolic bone disorder causes soft, vulnerable bones and may result in deformity to the tortoise's limbs.

Those scientific conditions are treatable by way of an exotics veterinarian who focuses on reptiles. Make certain to observe your vet's directions for care and treatment.